A QUICK & EASY GUIDE TO

CONSENT

WRITTEN & DRAWN BY **ISABELLA ROTMAN**

COLORS BY LUKE HOWARD

A LIMERENCE PRESS
PUBLICATION

PUBLISHED BY LIMERENCE PRESS

LIMERENCE PRESS IS AN IMPRINT OF ONI-LION FORGE PUBLISHING GROUP, LLC.

Written, Drawn & Lettered by
ISABELLA ROTMAN

Colors by
LUKE HOWARD

Cover illustration by
ISABELLA ROTMAN

Cover colors by
LUKE HOWARD

Designed by
KATE Z. STONE

Edited by
ARI YARWOOD
& **AMANDA MEADOWS**

LimerencePress.com
limerencepress
onipress

isabellarotman.com
this_might_hurt
IsabellaRotman

lukehoward.net
lukehwrd
LukeHwrd

First Edition: October 2020
ISBN 978-1-62010-794-2
eISBN 978-1-62010-815-4

Library of Congress Control Number: 2020932168

A QUICK & EASY GUIDE TO CONSENT, October 2020. Published by Limerence Press, an imprint of Oni-Lion Forge Publishing Group, LLC, 1319 SE M.L. King Jr. Blvd., Suite 240, Portland, OR 97214.

PRINTED IN CHINA.

10 9 8 7 6 5 4 3 2 1

Hi, and welcome to *A Quick & Easy Guide to Consent!* There are some things I want to mention before we get started.

CAUTION

Content Warning

Before we dig in, heads up that difficult topics will be covered here! We can't really talk about consent without taking about sexual violence, nor do we want to. Sexual violence is upsetting for anyone, especially survivors of trauma. **Please proceed with caution: this book will discuss the reality of sexual violence throughout, along with research and theory on it; but will not show visual depictions or graphic descriptions.**

Gender

Consent applies and matters equally to all genders. While many dynamics of sexual violence can follow gendered patterns, and we will discuss some of those, please know they are by no means universal. While a few quotes in this book refer to men as perpetrators, please don't take those quotes out of context. Someone's gender expression is not an indicator of their gender identity, nor is it an indicator of consent. **Remember that sexual violence and other forms of abuse can and do happen to all genders, and in all types of relationships.**

Informational Disclaimer

All views are that of the author, Isabella Rotman, who is not an all-knowing resource. I strongly encourage you to investigate multiple viewpoints on the topic of consent. A list of recommended resources is provided in the back of the book. As time passes, statistics and cultural understanding may as well (and we hope it does, in a good way!), so we encourage you to stay up to date.

Scope

This book is about consent and how to do it right. **This book does not cover:**

- Specific laws and policies governing consent, as they vary depending on your location
- Recovery for survivors of sexual violence
- How society can or should hold accountable and/or rehabilitate perpetrators of sexual violence in a way that would increase community safety
- How to fix this messed up world

We're kissing!
Oh my gosh!
It's finally happening!

Wait, is she into this?

She's kissing me back, that probably means she's okay with it.

I'm just going to put my hands here and see if she's okay with that...

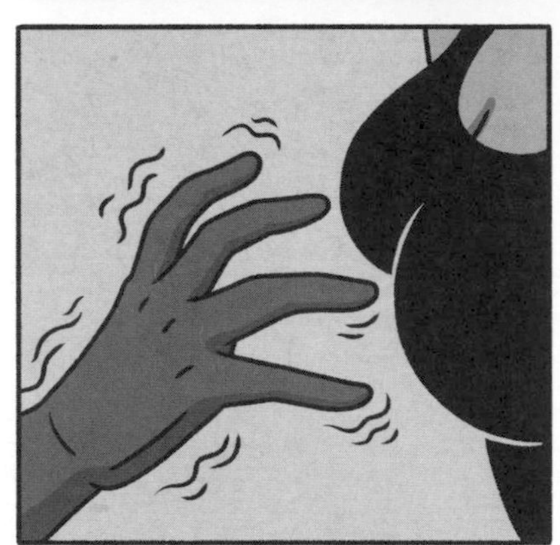

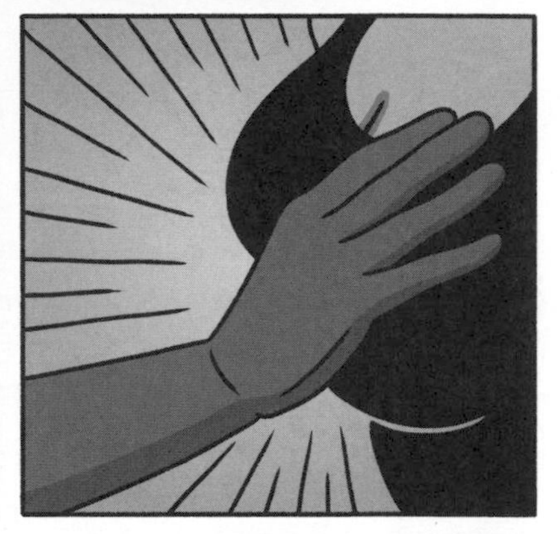

She didn't say no!
She was okay with it!

Yeah, that's a pretty recognizable scenario, isn't it?

Our friend Anthony here doesn't know what his partner wants, but he does know what he wants, so he's just going to keep doing different things until she says no.

And our friend Daniela here is put in the position of gatekeeper. At every new action her partner presents, she has to decide whether or not to reject him, never being given or taking the opportunity to say what she actually wants.

Well, I think we can do better than that, **can't we?!**
!!
!!

Who are you?
Why are you in my house?

Hi! I'm Sergeant Yes Means Yes from the Consent Cavalry. And I'd love to take a moment of your time to talk about affirmative consent.

Excuse me. I know how to say no to sex, and I could have sworn I locked the door...

Ah yes, but affirmative consent is so much more than that. Also, I'm not breaking and entering, because you see, I'm a magical guide, and all of us are fictional.

Sigh... Alright, **TELL US ABOUT CONSENT.**

Fantastic!
Teacher: Sergeant Yes Means Yes
Pronouns: They/them
Call me Sarge for short!
THE CONSENT CAVALRY

This is a class, but it is actually a book. A book to learn from and to give to people when they don't seem to "get it" and you're tired of explaining everything yourself.
And this book is about...
CONSENT

What is
CONSENT?

Consent is an explicitly communicated, reversible, mutual agreement made when all parties are capable of making that decision.
Do you want to _______?

Consent may or may not be verbal, but it has to be unambiguous and voluntary.
Yes!

In short, to consent is to communicate yes, with all your decision-making capabilities in functional order and full knowledge of what that "yes" means!

The word "**consent**" refers to any sort of agreement for something to happen.
Can I hug you?
Yes!

But these days, it is usually used in the context of sexual activity.
Do you wanna make out in my parents' car?
Heck yeah!
Throughout this book, when we say "consent," we mean consent in the context of sex or other physical or sexual contact.

Oh my gosh, did you not want me to do that stuff?
No, no! I did! I mean I never said that I did, and you never asked, and I'm not really into boob stuff... but I figured we would get to what I wanted to do eventually...

Yeah, and this is why it's best to ask directly.

Affirmative consent is about making sure that everyone involved in a sexual activity is **into it.** And when I say "into it," I don't mean "okay with it." I mean **INTO IT.**

When your mindset is that you only want to have sex with people who want to have sex with you, affirmative consent comes naturally.

Consent is not a hurdle you have to jump over to "get sex" from someone. It's the indispensable communication required for the collaborative process of doing something sexual, or really doing anything at all, with another person.

There is an area of danger that exists between the low bar of willingness, the line of consent most often reflected in law, and affirmative consent, the gold standard of consent I'm talking about in this book.

What happens in this gray space centers around one person prioritizing their own wants over the wants and needs of their partner, and making it their goal to convince their partner to comply with those wants.

These acts are selfish, usually involve emotional coercion, and can cause deep, lasting pain.

This has been culturally taught to many of us. Gender dynamics, while far from universal, cannot be ignored in this conversation.

Many young men have been taught that sex is a game where the man pursues and the women concedes, if he is smart, attractive, or persistent enough to convince her to do so.

Young women are taught that it is their job to withhold, and are discouraged from thinking about what they want to do, only what they allow men to do with them.

From this dynamic we get the *"no means no"* model of consent, where the man pursues until the woman says no, at which point he, a gentlemen, stops physical activity, but continues to pester.

That's kind of **sexist**—

Yes, it absolutely is sexist. It assumes heteronormative relationships as well.
For those of us who aren't straight, or don't fall neatly into one of the categories of man or woman, the message is less clear.

But affirmative consent isn't like that. There aren't roles prescribed by gender.

Everyone gets to ask, everyone gets to suggest, and everyone gets to respond.

Now, I don't want to come across as saying that all people who commit acts of sexual violence are just "misunderstanding" consent. Most perpetrators of sexual assault fully admit that what they did was not consensual, though they often deny that it was rape at the same time.

Most studies agree that the majority of perpetrators of sexual violence are experts at rationalizing their behavior. They will find some way to believe a false notion that excuses their behavior and avoids accountability.
This is a type of cognitive distortion.

All that being said, we get to decide what kind of person we want to be!

The ideas that perpetrators of sexual violence use to rationalize their actions grow out of culture.

NOD
I truly believe that if we commit to listening to and valuing our partners' wants and boundaries both in and outside of sex, we can create a new culture where sexual assault and harassment is no longer tolerated, and the sexuality of all genders is celebrated.

Quote From a Sexual Consent Educator

"We have the power to dream up and manifest something far better than merely being able to say no and to say yes: something which is an entirely different animal than scenarios which are positive primarily because they have avoided the most negative consequences or results. Good sex, great sex, and enriching sexuality are not just about the absence of physical or emotional pain nor only about emotional intimacy. They are about desire and the full expression of that desire."
- Heather Corinna, "An Immodest Proposal"

Sex is, and can be, so many things. Before one engages in any of it, wouldn't you want to set the stage to make it the most rewarding experience it could be for everyone involved?
Yeah!
Of course!

At Its Core
CONSENT IS SIMPLE

Sex, like the people involved in it, is complicated.

And often when we talk about sex, we can get bogged down in the very complicated intersection of communication and desire.

But at the heart of it, **affirmative consent** is strikingly simple.

Does this person **want** to have **this type of sex with me,**
and
are they **capable** of **making that decision** right now?

Whenever the variables start to feel overwhelming, pause.
Push past all the complicating factors, and return to this simple core concept.

If you prioritize your boundaries and desires, and the boundaries and desires of your partner as being equally important and respected, consent isn't hard. It's fun, hot, and it goes way beyond "yes" and "no."

I want us to think of "okay with it," or willingness to have sex, as the lowest bar of consent.

Any sexual activity without willingness from all people involved is sexual assault. Period.

Maybe you've heard this before. Maybe it feels intuitive, in which case, great!

Maybe this feels like a revolutionary idea, because for some of us, especially those of us who are not cisgender men, just finding a partner who seeks out and supports our willingness is a big deal.

But I encourage all of us to set a standard beyond that. **Affirmative consent** isn't just about whether your partner does or doesn't want to have sex with you. It's **about discussing what kind(s) of sex you want to have, respecting your partner's boundaries and desires, and advocating for your own.**

Let's look at some examples!
Affirma
Conse

I'm talking about a **CLEARLY COMMUNICATED YES!**
I'd really like to kiss you now.
Yes, please!!!

It's when everyone involved wants to keep doing what they are doing...
Can I touch you here?
Girl, yes.

...and continue to want to keep doing it the whole time!
Do you want me to keep feeling you up?
Absolutely.

While there are many ways to communicate consent, it's good to get in the practice of asking directly, and answering directly. You are not a mindreader, and you shouldn't expect your partner to be.
Do they... want... to... have sex... with me...

So, let's do a little quiz.
If you ask, and someone answers yes,
that's consent! If you ask, and...

THE PERSON PRETENDS NOT TO HEAR YOU...

...GIVES AN AMBIVALENT ANSWER...

...OR CHANGES THE SUBJECT.

Would you like me to go down on you?
OH GEE, I WONDER WHAT'S NEW ON NETFLIX.

Oh yeah, that's definitely a no.

Correct. Anything other than a yes is a no.

Okay, but Sarge... what if you think you're into something, but then it's happening, and you realize that you aren't?

What happens then?

That's a really great question. Consent is ongoing, and can be reversed at any time.
So, I could just change my mind? He could just change his mind?

Yes, essentially. Anyone can "just change their mind" at any time. Consent isn't something we do once, it's something we do or don't do, and continue to do or not do, for the entirety of a sexual interaction.

On that same train of thought, sometimes a person might not know exactly if they want something or not, but they want to explore the possibility of it, knowing they have the safety to stop at any time.
Would you like to roleplay as sexy vampires?
I want to try it out... but I'm not sure how much I'll like it. Let's go slow to start.

That's kind of scary.

What if my partner changes their mind and doesn't tell me?

As things escalate, check in with your partner.
If you notice a change in body language, such as your partner stiffening, no longer engaging with you, or turning away, take that as a cue to pause and talk to them.

Just because someone was into one thing doesn't mean they will be into something else. Consent is an ongoing conversation.

Right! When it comes to consent, always err on the side of caution. When in doubt, ask.

What Is Sex?

An important thing to remember here is that **sex isn't just one thing.**

Often, when people say **"sex,"** they mean penis-in-vagina genital intercourse.

Well, that's quite a narrow view of sex, and doesn't reflect the breadth of ways most people express their sexuality together!

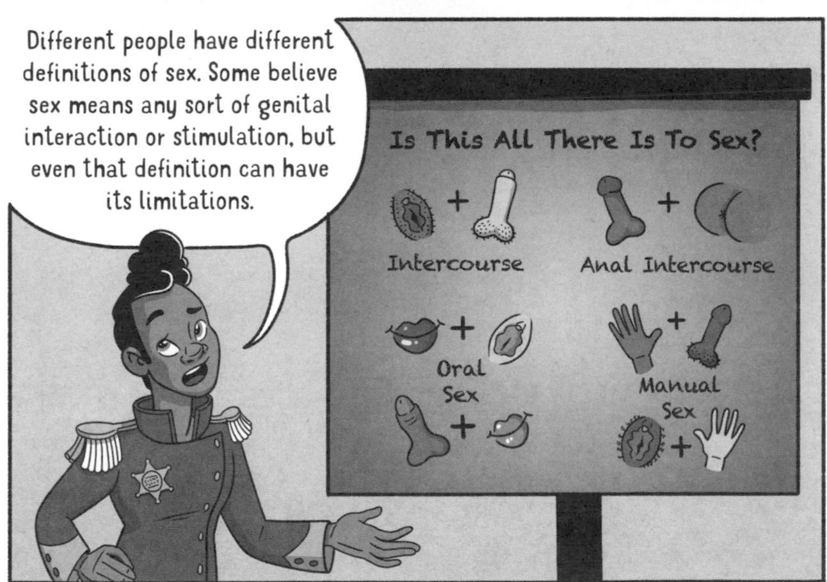
Different people have different definitions of sex. Some believe sex means any sort of genital interaction or stimulation, but even that definition can have its limitations.
Is This All There Is To Sex?
Intercourse
Anal Intercourse
Oral Sex
Manual Sex

In this book, when we say someone is having sex or doing something sexual with another person, we mean they are acting on their sexuality! Which could be any number of things...

Like...
Mutual masturbation!

Dry humping. That's like... rubbing your genitals together, with clothes on.*

*Technichally called **frottage.**

Scissoring.*

*Tribbing.** Rubbing vulvas together. Sometimes this is much more vulva on thigh.

Finger stuff: handjobs, fingering, fisting...*

***Manual-genital sex**

Oral.* Going down on someone, or giving someone a blowjob.

***Oral-genital sex** (to/with a penis, vulva, or anus)

Using a **sex toy*** on another person.

*Vibrators, dildos, butt plugs, masturbation sleeves, and more

BUTT STUFF*!
*Anal sex, anal intercourse with a penis, toy, or hands

Sexting*... talking dirty... phone sex... you know.
?
*Virtual exchange of sexual words and/or images

Yes.... and probably other things, depending on what you're into!

So, with all of those things, think of sex as an ever-evolving and ever-changing series of interactions.

Consent is a state both of you must be in to move through these interactions.
STATE OF CONSENT

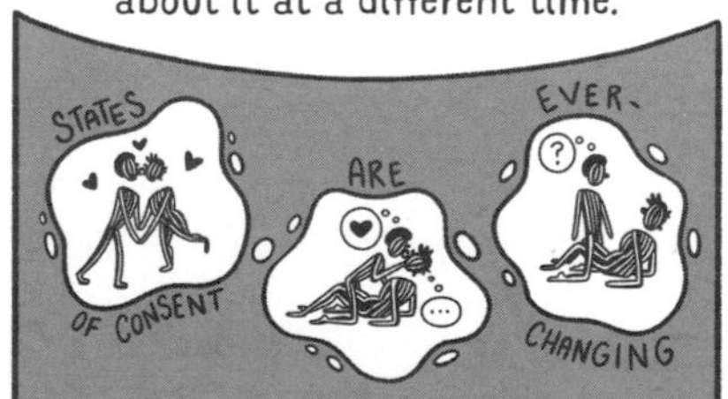
How each of you feels about each action may be different from other actions, or different from how you felt about it at a different time.
STATES OF CONSENT
ARE
EVER-CHANGING
?

Feelings changing is normal. Check in with each other and make sure each action is something both of you want in that moment.
STOP
?

But Sarge... Wouldn't asking someone what they want you to do with them
ruin the mood?
Actually,
I think it could be really hot.

It's true. When people are into what they're doing together, talking about it only tends to make it more sexy, not less.
I really liked the kissing. Did you like—
YES!
I mean... yeah. It was nice.
You're a good kisser.

Sometimes people are reluctant to ask because it gives their partner a bigger opportunity to say no.
Well, everyone SHOULD have a big opportunity to say no.
Everyone has different ideas of sexy, but what is definitely NOT SEXY is putting someone in a sexual situation who doesn't want to be there.

Tell Them What TURNS YOU ON!

Other times, though, people are reluctant to ask directly because they are nervous and unaccustomed to saying sexual things out loud. That makes total sense! **Talking about sex is a skill,** one you can work on and get more comfortable with. **The best sex happens when you can communicate what you like to your partner,** even if it's awkward or hard.

Try some of these phrases to help you get started!

I really love it when...
There's something I'd like to try...
I think it would be super sexy if...
I think it's really hot when you...
What you're doing feels good, but it'd feel even better if...
I have this fantasy about...

To help you brainstorm even more, we included a checklist in the back of this book!

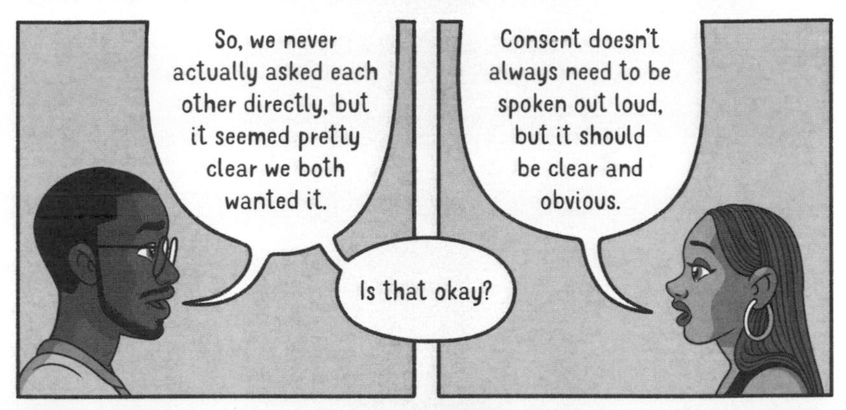

Quote From a Sexual Consent Educator

"Real consent requires us to really be present when we're having sex with someone. It requires us to see our sex partners – whether they be anonymous hookups or life partners – not simply as instrumental to our own pleasure but as co-equal collaborators, equally human and important, equally harmable, equally free and equally sovereign."

- Jaclyn Friedman, "Sex & Consent, It's Time to Go Beyond the Rules"

It's true that consent can be communicated without a direct question and answer.
So... Will you kiss me again?
NOD
A nod yes could be consent. Pulling someone closer could be consent. Asking someone if they have a condom could be consent.
Consent doesn't **have to be** communicated with words, but **if you are at all unsure**, you **need** to **stop and ask.**
Generally, non-verbal consent is only okay between people who have built trust and feel very comfortable with each other.

This is usually only the case for repeat partners who communicate well, are confident they can read each other's subtle cues, and have explicitly discussed that they are comfortable using body language and gestures to communicate consent.

However, if the person **doesn't respond with words OR with affirmative body language,** that is **NOT** consent.

You should be comfortable asking directly, and in most cases, it is best to ask directly. If you are at all unsure what someone's body language is communicating, pause, take a mental step back, and use your words!
Can I?
Uh-huh.
What about this?
Yes!

Well, these two seem to get it!
How about...
Yes!
and do you like...
Yeah... but lower.
That's it.
YES!

There's a bar downstairs.

Let's see

if

anyone

needs
our
help
SOME BAR
here!

While we're here, let's take a minute to go over a few things that definitely...
HAVE NOTHING to do with CONSENT!

APPEARANCE
Clearly, what I am wearing, how I dance, or what I happen to look like has nothing to do with whether or not I want to sleep with you.

PRIOR CONSENT
So what if I wanted it before? That doesn't mean I do now!

RELATIONSHIP STATUS
You don't get to assume you're entitled to sex with me just because we are dating.

GENDER
Just because I'm a man doesn't mean I want it all the time. Do you think men are all dirty horndogs who ALWAYS want to get laid?

OR BEING A SEX WORKER
Excuse me, nothing about my job means my boundaries don't need to be respected. Sex workers have the same right to consent that anyone else does.

None of these things tell you anything about whether or not, and what kind of sex is on the table.

The only thing that "tells you" that is asking.

CONSENT MUST BE FREELY GIVEN!

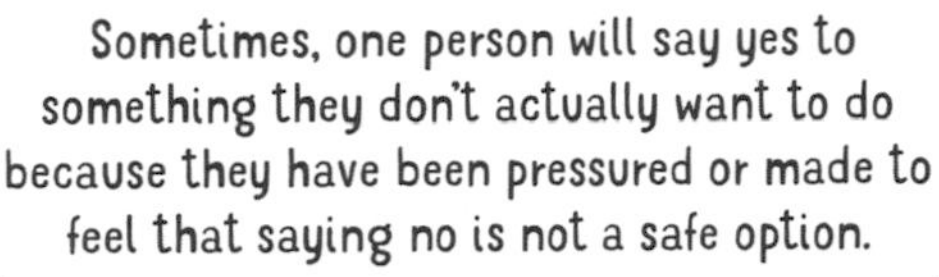
Sometimes, one person will say yes to something they don't actually want to do because they have been pressured or made to feel that saying no is not a safe option.
This is called **coercion.** Here are a few examples.

I bought you dinner and took you out and you're not even going to come up to my place? Come on.
GUILT/ OBLIGATION

But you know how emotionally unstable I am. If you were to reject me in any way, who knows how I might react!
EMOTIONAL MANIPULATION

But I'm influental, rich, and have the ability to positively or negatively affect your career. Are you sure you want to say no to me?
LEVERAGING POWER

What is important to remember here is that **NO ONE OWES SEX TO ANYONE ELSE, EVER.**

Sex is not a commodity that anyone is ever obligated to trade in reciprocation for anything else.

If anyone attempts to make you believe that you owe them sex for any reason, that means they feel **entitled to your body.**

And **no one** is entitled to your body but **yourself.**

A "yes" is not consent if it is made out of fear, or if the person is being manipulated or misled.

In order for consent to flourish, everyone must feel that their "no's," or "let's talk about it more's" will be comfortably respected.

Quote From a Sexual Consent Educator

"Your strong and solid no makes way for your deep, authentic yes. I was taught this late in life: "No is a complete sentence." You don't have to say no apologetically, and you don't have to explain your no. By practicing your no, you will cultivate a yes that is rooted in having agency, having power, and having respect for your own boundaries."

- Adrienne Maree Brown, "Reclaiming the Pleasure of Consent"

Sex educator Emily Nagoski sets up consent as two fundamental questions:
Does the person want to give consent, which we just covered,
and is the person
CAPABLE OF GIVING CONSENT?

Oh like, if a person is asleep, they can't consent.
Right.

Or underage.
NOD
Yes.

Or like... under some sort of love spell.

Susan... that was a joke, right?
Yes, Kai.

And on that note, if someone is **intoxicated**, they don't have the judgement to make a clear, informed decision.

Excuse me, General Funny Jacket.

Is it really sexual assault to have sex with someone who's been drinking?
I feel like people have drunk sex all the time.

In order to consent, you have to be capable of communicating and making a decision.
There are different levels of how drunk a person is.
At a certain level of intoxication, your ability to do these things is affected.

I agree with that, but there are still levels of drunk or high when you can totally make that kind of decision.

You're telling me that it's literally impossible to get tipsy and have consensual sex?

No, that's not what I'm saying.
Hmmm.

If a person's decision-making capabilities are intact, they are capable of making the decision to consent. If they are too drunk to think or speak clearly, or are passed out, there is absolutely no way they are capable of agreeing to sex.

Susan, what about consenting before we drink, when both of us are sober?

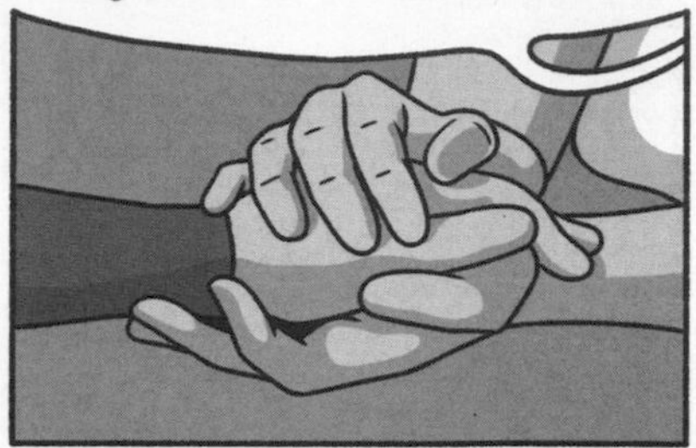
If we are considering drinking and then sleeping together, we can talk about it **before we start drinking** to figure out where both of us are at.

Yes! That sounds okay to me. As long as you **check back in**. And, **if one of you changes your mind**, you should both be willing and able to **stop what you are doing** despite your intoxication.

The ugly truth about intoxication is that it **impairs our ability to advocate for ourselves, judge situations, and react appropriately.**
Because of this, it's **hard to judge and be realistic about your (or someone else's) ability to do these things when you are intoxicated.**

If you plan on being intoxicated and sexual at the same time, it's important to talk about it before you are intoxicated, be careful, and bring all of your empathy and consideration for your potential partner with you.

In any situation, if you are at all unsure that either your partner or yourself is **CAPABLE** of saying yes in that moment due to intoxication or another factor, **take a pause.**
Talk about it later.
No one is being hurt by **not** having sex right now.

AGE OF CONSENT

One factor that can legally affect one's ability to consent is **age.**

Children and underage teens are **not** considered developmentally able to give consent. There is also an **inequal power-dynamic** that exists between adults and minors.

In most countries, an **adult engaging in sexual behaviors with someone under the age of consent** will be treated as **criminal sexual conduct,** referred to as **statutory rape.**

Some age of consent laws include **"close-in-age exceptions"** which decriminalize consensual sex between one or more participants who are under the age of consent, **when the participants are significantly close in age.**
Close-in-age-exceptions are often called "Romeo and Juliet" policies.

...but soft, what light through yonder window breaks?

The legal age of consent and the laws surrounding it vary in different countries and states.

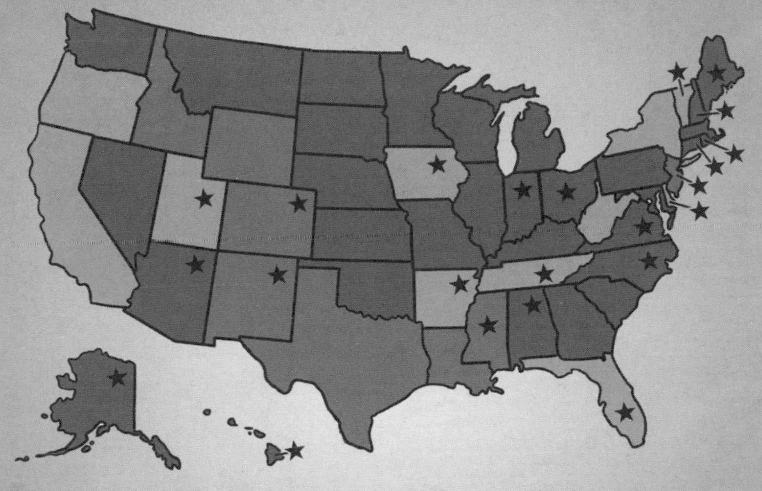

■ Age of Consent is 16
■ Age of Consent is 17
□ Age of Consent is 18
★ Close Age Exception

*Age of Consent in US states as of January 2020 via www.ageofconsent.net. Information may change by the time you read this. If **you are a teen using this information for your own reference, PLEASE check www.ageofconsent.net/states for up-to-date information.**

In Canada, the age of consent is 16, with close-in-age exceptions. **In the United States, laws vary state to state,** but the age of consent is always set between 16 and 18.

In states without a close-in-age exception, anyone under the age of consent is legally unable to consent with anyone, even if they are very close in age.
What, really? My partner is less than one year older than me!

First of all, how did you get in here? Hand over your fake ID.

Thank you.

If you and/or your partner are under 18, I strongly advise you not take, text, or email sexually explicit photos.
NUDES

TAKING OR EXCHANGING
SEXY PICS
IS OKAY FOR
ADULTS
OVER THE AGE OF 18
ONLY
Laws vary depending on location, but when nude or sexual photos involve minors, most states consider this **child pornography**, which is a **felony**, and could get you and/or your sexting partner in a **lot of trouble.** This is true even if all participants consider the photos and the exchange consensual.

Even if I am taking a photo of myself?
Yes.

And sending it to someone my same age??
Yes.

And there are no adults involved at all???
Yes.

I have some questions about the fairness of certain age of consent laws.

I thought you might. While age of consent laws may not always be fair or always sound, they can protect young people from predatory adults.

An adult coercing an underage person into sex is **never, ever okay.**
TAXI

The partner that is younger than the age of consent is not breaking the law in these cases, the older partner is.

TAXI

When used as a protection, these laws can help underage people seek justice when they were coerced by an adult with more power, agency, and resources than they have.

These laws may seem complicated,
but what is legally relevant to you is your SPECIFIC area.
You can look up your local age of consent laws at
www.ageofconsent.net

TAXI

IS EVERYONE FULLY INFORMED?

Another instance where someone would be incapable of giving consent is if they are not **fully informed.** If you aspire to do something sexual with someone else, then it's your responsibility to communicate all relevant information.

STI (SEXUALY TRANSMITTED INFECTION) STATUS AND RISKS

Just so you know, I have herpes simplex 2 on my genitals. I'm not having an outbreak now, and have plenty of dental dams.

Thank you for telling me!

I'm going to read up about herpes before I come over tonight.

CONTRACEPTION (IF THIS APPLIES TO YOU AND YOUR PARTNER)
I'm on birth control pills, but I prefer that we use condoms as well, for extra safety and to protect from STIs.
Sounds good to me! Do you have a condom preference?
LUBE

ANY OTHER RELEVANT INFORMATION
Before this goes further, I want to let you know that I'm in an open relationship.
Are you open to talking about that?

While it is everyone's responsibility to freely offer this information in situations where it is relevant, you shouldn't be afraid to ask for it as well.

EMOTIONAL CONSIDERATIONS COULD INCLUDE:

WHAT WORDS YOU USE FOR YOURSELF AND BODY

There are certain words that I use for my gender and my body parts. Can I share those with you, and ask what words you use?

BOUNDARIES IN RELATION TO PAST TRAUMA

Certain positions remind me of something bad that happened to me, so I'd like to avoid them.

RELATIONSHIP STATUS

Before we do anything else, I'd really like to know how we feel about each other. Are you down to talk about that?

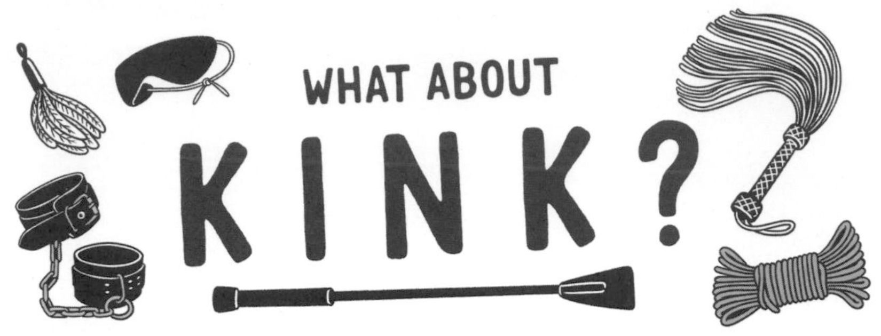
WHAT ABOUT
KINK?

Ohh, this date seems to be going well.

Hey Sarge, how does consent work if you're into... kinkier stuff?

In some kink situations, it's hard to communicate because of gags or other barriers.

And in some situations, saying no is part of it!

If you agree to be submissive, does that mean you've agreed to other things?

Often partners in kink will discuss what they want to do before ever getting intimate, so that they both go in fully aware of each other's yucks and yums.

If saying no is part of the scene, partners will decide on a **safeword** to communicate if they want to stop.

And if someone is wearing a gag or is unable to speak for another reason, the safeword can take the form of a physical cue.

Consent is reversible and fully informed in kink just like it is anywhere else. You tell each other what you want to do and don't want to do, and if someone says they want to stop, then you stop.

FEAR OF REJECTION

What if I want to ask for what I want...
...but I'm afraid of getting **rejected?**

Sometimes we want to avoid putting ourselves in situations where there is a risk of being told no, but when we do this, we end up missing out big time!

While a "no" is final and to be respected, it is not a reflection on your worth.

A "no" means "not that, and not right now." That's it.

I feel like there's a lot more to a "no" than that...
But those meanings usually come from our own insecurities, not the other person.

So my advice is to try getting used to hearing "no," and feeling okay with it!

f someone were to say...

No, I don't want a slice of pie right now.

We wouldn't assume they meant...

No, I **hate** pie and also you and I will **never** eat pie or any other baked good with you **now** or **ever**!

Now, sex is a lot more loaded than pie (for most people), but the basic premise is the same.

Just because someone doesn't want pie with you right now, doesn't mean that you are a bad person who is not worthy of pie.

Maybe they'd rather have cake, instead.

Or start with cookies, and work up to pie.

Or, maybe they really just don't want to eat dessert with you for whatever reason, and that's fine, too.

MAKE IT ABOUT YOU

WHAT? I worked **SO HARD** on this pie. My pie is the **BEST PIE** and I **DIDN'T WANT TO SHARE IT WITH YOU ANYWAY.**

REFUSE TO ACCEPT THE ANSWER

Oh, but what about just a **really small** piece of pie? I bet you'll really like it. I can tell you want pie.

OR FEEL GUILTY FOR ASKING THE QUESTION

Oh my gosh I'm **so sorry** I'll never ask again I can't believe I offered you pie let's pretend it didn't happen.

Instead, immediately accept their answer, and appreciate their honesty.

Often, it is best at this point to figure out the context of the "no."

Immediate negative reactions are an abrupt stop.

Consent, like dessert, is a conversation. The only way you know what someone wants is to ASK.

Can I take your shirt off?
Uhhh... I don't think so.
That's okay! Would you like to talk about it more?

THE
CONSENT
CAVALRY

IN REVIEW...

Consent is an **explicitly communicated, reversible, mutual agreement made when all parties are capable of making that decision.**
Consent may or may not be verbal, but it has to be **unambiguous** and **voluntary.**

Sex is and can be many things. Any sexual interaction is an ever-evolving and changing series of actions. Consent is a state both of you must be in to move through these interactions.
Therefore, as actions change, or if your partner's reactions change, **check in.**

Sexual assault is **never** the fault of the person who was assaulted.
Sexaul assault is squarely the fault of whoever chose to not respect another person's boundaries.

ALRIGHT, so let's go over what we've learned!

A person is **not capable** of making the decision to consent sexually if they are **asleep, unconscious, under the age of consent** (specifics vary depending on local laws), or **their judgment is impaired by drugs and alcohol.**

Consent must be **voluntary** and **fully informed.**
If a person says yes to sex **under false pretenses, or influenced by threats or coercion, that is not consent.**

You're going to have better sex and better relationships if you **communicate** what you'd like to do with who you'd like to do it with!
Even if it's scary!

I know this all can seem really complicated, but just remember if you ever get unsure, the core concept of affirmative consent is simple.

Does this person **want** to have this type of sex with with me,

and are they **capable** of making that decision right now?

If you are ever unsure about either of those points, take a step back.

Consider your desires and boundaries. Consider the desires and boundaries of your partner(s).

And talk to
each other.
SOME BAR

☐ YES ☐ NO ☐ MAYBE SO CHECKLIST

A "Yes, No, Maybe So" checklist is a list boundaries, activities, and considerations for the kinds of sex **YOU** want to have! You can use this list as a self-reflection exercise to get a gauge on what you're interested in. You could also share it with your partner(s), assuming you trust them with so much personal information, to see where your interests overlap. Nothing you mark on this list is a commitment, just an idea of how you generally feel. It's worth coming back to this list every once in a while. What you like today might be different tomorrow!

Communication

I am comfortable with:

- ☐ Consent using words
- ☐ Consent that doesn't involve words, such as moaning, and body language.
- ☐ Guiding hands and bodies in what they are doing, and vice versa.
- ☐ Initiating or having sex while or after I have been using alcohol or other recreational drugs. If yes, please discuss boundaries here: ______________
- ☐ Establishing a safeword. If yes, my safeword is: ______________

What words and phrases do you like to use for things?

My pronouns are: ______________

I want my gender to be referred to as: ______________

I want my sexual orientation to be referred to as: ______________

I want my genitals to be referred to as: ______________

I want my chest to be referred to as: ______________

Do you have any accessibility needs or considerations that you would like potential sexual partner(s) to know about? ______________

Safer Sex: Contraception

Sex is never totally risk-free, and different types of sex come with different risks. **If you are unfamiliar with safer sex practices, please take the time to visit Scarleteen.com for free, comprehensive and medically accurate info on managing risks in sex, or another resource in the back of this book!**

If you have the types of sex that can result in pregnancy, are you interested in using contraceptives to prevent pregnancy?

☐ Yes ☐ No ☐ This does not apply to the type of sex I am having or planning on having

IF YES, WHICH METHOD(S) OF CONTRACEPTION WOULD YOU LIKE TO USE OR ARE ALREADY USING?

Condoms

☐ Would like to use
☐ Already using

Internal Condoms

☐ Would like to use
☐ Already using

Cervical Barriers
Diaphragms & Cervical Caps

☐ Would like to use
☐ Already using

The Pill
Oral Contraceptives

☐ Would like to use
☐ Already using

Vaginal Ring

☐ Would like to use
☐ Already using

The Implant

☐ Would like to use
☐ Already using

The Patch

☐ Would like to use
☐ Already using

The Shot
Depo-Provera

☐ Would like to use
☐ Already using

Hormonal IUD

☐ Would like to use
☐ Already using

Copper IUD

☐ Would like to use
☐ Already using

Fertility Charting
Not Recommended as Sole Contraceptive Method

☐ Would like to use
☐ Already using

Withdrawal
Not Recommended as Sole Contraceptive Method

EVICTION NOTICE

☐ Would like to use
☐ Already using

Safer Sex: STI Risk Reduction

For sexual activities where the transmission of STIs is possible, please mark which methods you want to use to make sex safer by checking the box for **always, sometimes, or never.** If you don't plan on having the type of sex requiring this type of protection, you can check **N/A** for not applicable.

Using condoms for vaginal intercourse

- ☐ Always
- ☐ Sometimes
- ☐ Never
- ☐ N/A

Using condoms for anal intercourse

- ☐ Always
- ☐ Sometimes
- ☐ Never
- ☐ N/A

Using condoms for oral sex

- ☐ Always
- ☐ Sometimes
- ☐ Never
- ☐ N/A

Using dental dams for oral sex

- ☐ Always
- ☐ Sometimes
- ☐ Never
- ☐ N/A

Using condoms and dental dams for shared sex toys

- ☐ Always
- ☐ Sometimes
- ☐ Never
- ☐ N/A

Using gloves for manual sex, anal or vaginal

- ☐ Always
- ☐ Sometimes
- ☐ Never
- ☐ N/A

Taking Pe-Exposure Prophylaxis (PrEP) to reduce risk of HIV transmission

- ☐ Always
- ☐ Never
- ☐ N/A

Getting tested for STIs

More questions on next page

- ☐ Multiple times a year
- ☐ Yearly
- ☐ Every few years
- ☐ Never

How often do you want to be tested for STIs?

☐ Every 3 Months ☐ Every 3-6 Months ☐ Every 6-12 Months ☐ Yearly ☐ Every Few Years ☐ Never

How often do you want your partner(s) to be tested for STIs?

☐ Every 3 Months ☐ Every 3-6 Months ☐ Every 6-12 Months ☐ Yearly ☐ Every Few Years ☐ Never

Are you comfortable disclosing results of STI testing with partner(s)?

☐ Yes ☐ No ☐ That depends: ____________________

____

Materials

Do you have any allergies or sensitivities to latex or other materials used in safer sex supplies?

____

____

Do you prefer certain kinds of lube?

____

____

Are you sensitive or allergic to any ingredients used in lube?

____

____

A LITTLE INFO ABOUT DIFFERENT TYPES OF LUBE!			
Water-Based	**Silicone-Based**	**Hybrid**	**Oil-Based**
The most versatile lube. Safe to use with condoms and sex toys. Not very long lasting.	Very long lasting. Safe to use with condoms. Can damage silicone or silicone-based sex toys.	Safe to use with condoms, usually safe to use with silicone toys, depending on the brand.	Should NOT BE USED WITH CONDOMS because it can break them down. Not recommended for vaginal use because it is associated with higher rates of infection.

Are there any other safer sex considerations you would like to talk about?

____

____

____

____

____

Activities

This is a list of activities that you may or may not be interested in. Read through the list and mark off which things are a definite **"Yes, I'm into that!"**, a definite **"No, I am NOT into that,"** or more of a **"Maybe, I'm not sure."** If it's something you like thinking about, but probably wouldn't want to do in real life, mark off **fantasy**. If you don't feel like an activity applies to you, you're are welcome to leave it unmarked.

Please note that many sex acts come with varying degrees of risk, which can be reduced with appropriate research, communication and care. A list of sex education resources is provided in the back of this book to help you get informed!

Physical	
Masturbation (alone)	☐ Yes ☐ Maybe ☐ No ☐ Fantasy
Cuddling/nonsexual touching	☐ Yes ☐ Maybe ☐ No ☐ Fantasy
Kissing on the mouth	☐ Yes ☐ Maybe ☐ No ☐ Fantasy
Mutual masturbation	☐ Yes ☐ Maybe ☐ No ☐ Fantasy
Dry humping Rubbing genitals together or on thigh with clothes on	☐ Yes ☐ Maybe ☐ No ☐ Fantasy
Dry humping, naked Rubbing genitals or on thigh without clothes	☐ Yes ☐ Maybe ☐ No ☐ Fantasy
Scissoring Rubbing vulvas together	☐ Yes ☐ Maybe ☐ No ☐ Fantasy

	GIVING	RECEIVING
Massage on back, shoulders, or legs	☐ Yes ☐ Maybe ☐ No ☐ Fantasy	☐ Yes ☐ Maybe ☐ No ☐ Fantasy
Touching chest or breast(s)	☐ Yes ☐ Maybe ☐ No ☐ Fantasy	☐ Yes ☐ Maybe ☐ No ☐ Fantasy
Kissing on neck, shoulders, or back	☐ Yes ☐ Maybe ☐ No ☐ Fantasy	☐ Yes ☐ Maybe ☐ No ☐ Fantasy

Physical (Continued)	GIVING	RECEIVING
Kissing on the chest or breast(s)	☐ Yes ☐ Maybe ☐ No ☐ Fantasy	☐ Yes ☐ Maybe ☐ No ☐ Fantasy
Hickies/activities that leave marks If yes, discuss where and how hard.	☐ Yes ☐ Maybe ☐ No ☐ Fantasy	☐ Yes ☐ Maybe ☐ No ☐ Fantasy
Watching or being watched while masturbating	☐ Yes ☐ Maybe ☐ No ☐ Fantasy	☐ Yes ☐ Maybe ☐ No ☐ Fantasy
Manual Sex: Hands on a penis/testicle(s)	☐ Yes ☐ Maybe ☐ No ☐ Fantasy	☐ Yes ☐ Maybe ☐ No ☐ Fantasy
Manual Sex: Hands on vulva	☐ Yes ☐ Maybe ☐ No ☐ Fantasy	☐ Yes ☐ Maybe ☐ No ☐ Fantasy
Manual Sex: Fingers inside vagina	☐ Yes ☐ Maybe ☐ No ☐ Fantasy	☐ Yes ☐ Maybe ☐ No ☐ Fantasy
Manual Sex: Vaginal fisting	☐ Yes ☐ Maybe ☐ No ☐ Fantasy	☐ Yes ☐ Maybe ☐ No ☐ Fantasy
Manual Sex: Fingers on anus	☐ Yes ☐ Maybe ☐ No ☐ Fantasy	☐ Yes ☐ Maybe ☐ No ☐ Fantasy
Manual Sex: Fingers inside rectum	☐ Yes ☐ Maybe ☐ No ☐ Fantasy	☐ Yes ☐ Maybe ☐ No ☐ Fantasy
Manual Sex: Anal fisting	☐ Yes ☐ Maybe ☐ No ☐ Fantasy	☐ Yes ☐ Maybe ☐ No ☐ Fantasy
Oral Sex: Tongue or mouth on vulva	☐ Yes ☐ Maybe ☐ No ☐ Fantasy	☐ Yes ☐ Maybe ☐ No ☐ Fantasy
Oral Sex: Tongue or mouth on penis and/or testicle(s)	☐ Yes ☐ Maybe ☐ No ☐ Fantasy	☐ Yes ☐ Maybe ☐ No ☐ Fantasy
Oral Sex/Rimming: Tongue or mouth on anus	☐ Yes ☐ Maybe ☐ No ☐ Fantasy	☐ Yes ☐ Maybe ☐ No ☐ Fantasy
Vaginal Intercourse	☐ Yes ☐ Maybe ☐ No ☐ Fantasy	☐ Yes ☐ Maybe ☐ No ☐ Fantasy
Anal Intercourse	☐ Yes ☐ Maybe ☐ No ☐ Fantasy	☐ Yes ☐ Maybe ☐ No ☐ Fantasy

Physical (Continued)	GIVING	RECEIVING
Scratching Please discuss where, and how hard.	☐ Yes ☐ Maybe ☐ No ☐ Fantasy	☐ Yes ☐ Maybe ☐ No ☐ Fantasy
"Talking dirty" before, during, and/or after sex	☐ Yes ☐ Maybe ☐ No ☐ Fantasy	☐ Yes ☐ Maybe ☐ No ☐ Fantasy
Spanking with hand Please discuss where and how hard.	☐ Yes ☐ Maybe ☐ No ☐ Fantasy	☐ Yes ☐ Maybe ☐ No ☐ Fantasy
Sex with more than one partner at the same time There is a wide range of options here, please discuss specifics and safety.	☐ Yes ☐ Maybe ☐ No ☐ Fantasy	

Not Necessarily Physical		
Disclosing sex or a relationship you are in with other people	☐ Yes ☐ Maybe ☐ No ☐ Fantasy	
"Talking dirty" on the phone	☐ Yes ☐ Maybe ☐ No ☐ Fantasy	
"Talking dirty" over text	☐ Yes ☐ Maybe ☐ No ☐ Fantasy	
Video-chat sex	☐ Yes ☐ Maybe ☐ No ☐ Fantasy	
Role playing (please discuss what)	☐ Yes ☐ Maybe ☐ No ☐ Fantasy	
Watching porn with a partner	☐ Yes ☐ Maybe ☐ No ☐ Fantasy	
Reading erotica with a partner	☐ Yes ☐ Maybe ☐ No ☐ Fantasy	
	GIVING	RECEIVING
Sending/receiving nude or explicit photographs	☐ Yes ☐ Maybe ☐ No ☐ Fantasy	☐ Yes ☐ Maybe ☐ No ☐ Fantasy

Sex Toys	SOLO	GIVING	RECIEVING
Using a vibrator externally on the clitoris, vulva, nipples, anus and/or perineum	☐ Yes ☐ No	☐ Yes ☐ Maybe ☐ No ☐ Fantasy	☐ Yes ☐ Maybe ☐ No ☐ Fantasy
Using a vibrator internally (vaginal)	☐ Yes ☐ No	☐ Yes ☐ Maybe ☐ No ☐ Fantasy	☐ Yes ☐ Maybe ☐ No ☐ Fantasy
Using a butt plug and/or vibrating butt plug	☐ Yes ☐ No	☐ Yes ☐ Maybe ☐ No ☐ Fantasy	☐ Yes ☐ Maybe ☐ No ☐ Fantasy
Using a dildo (vaginal)	☐ Yes ☐ No	☐ Yes ☐ Maybe ☐ No ☐ Fantasy	☐ Yes ☐ Maybe ☐ No ☐ Fantasy
Using a dildo (anal)	☐ Yes ☐ No	☐ Yes ☐ Maybe ☐ No ☐ Fantasy	☐ Yes ☐ Maybe ☐ No ☐ Fantasy
Using a strap-on (vaginal)		☐ Yes ☐ Maybe ☐ No ☐ Fantasy	☐ Yes ☐ Maybe ☐ No ☐ Fantasy
Using a strap-on (anal)		☐ Yes ☐ Maybe ☐ No ☐ Fantasy	☐ Yes ☐ Maybe ☐ No ☐ Fantasy
Oral sex on a dildo	☐ Yes ☐ No	☐ Yes ☐ Maybe ☐ No ☐ Fantasy	☐ Yes ☐ Maybe ☐ No ☐ Fantasy
Using a masturbation sleeve	☐ Yes ☐ No	☐ Yes ☐ Maybe ☐ No ☐ Fantasy	☐ Yes ☐ Maybe ☐ No ☐ Fantasy
Using cockrings and/or vibrating cockrings	☐ Yes ☐ No	☐ Yes ☐ Maybe ☐ No ☐ Fantasy	☐ Yes ☐ Maybe ☐ No ☐ Fantasy
Impact with tool Paddles, floggers, whips, etc. Discuss safety, where, and how hard.	☐ Yes ☐ No	☐ Yes ☐ Maybe ☐ No ☐ Fantasy	☐ Yes ☐ Maybe ☐ No ☐ Fantasy
Restraints Restricting movement with rope, cuffs, or other bondage gear. Discuss safety, where, and how.	☐ Yes ☐ No	☐ Yes ☐ Maybe ☐ No ☐ Fantasy	☐ Yes ☐ Maybe ☐ No ☐ Fantasy
Blindfolds Something that covers eyes and blocks vision	☐ Yes ☐ No	☐ Yes ☐ Maybe ☐ No ☐ Fantasy	☐ Yes ☐ Maybe ☐ No ☐ Fantasy

Anything Else?

There are a lot more activities and sex toys than what's on this list! Feel free to write in any other activities you would like to consider or discuss below.

Write In	GIVING	RECIEVING
	☐ Yes ☐ Maybe ☐ No ☐ Fantasy	☐ Yes ☐ Maybe ☐ No ☐ Fantasy
	☐ Yes ☐ Maybe ☐ No ☐ Fantasy	☐ Yes ☐ Maybe ☐ No ☐ Fantasy
	☐ Yes ☐ Maybe ☐ No ☐ Fantasy	☐ Yes ☐ Maybe ☐ No ☐ Fantasy
	☐ Yes ☐ Maybe ☐ No ☐ Fantasy	☐ Yes ☐ Maybe ☐ No ☐ Fantasy
	☐ Yes ☐ Maybe ☐ No ☐ Fantasy	☐ Yes ☐ Maybe ☐ No ☐ Fantasy
	☐ Yes ☐ Maybe ☐ No ☐ Fantasy	☐ Yes ☐ Maybe ☐ No ☐ Fantasy

What else turns you on?

____

____

Is there anything else you prefer **not** to do or discuss with a partner?

____

____

Do you like or need any sort of aftercare after sexual activity? If so, what?

____

____

I hope you enjoyed this checklist! Please note that this is by no means a comprehensive list of EVERY sexual thing that people do. Feel free to check out further lists on the resources page in the back of this book, seek some out yourself, or make one of your own!

BIBLIOGRAPHY

"Age of Consent & Sexual Abuse Laws Around the World." *AgeOfConsent.net*, www.ageofconsent.net/.

Bongiovanni, Archie. "Toys Are for Us: How to Start Using Sex Toys with a Partner." *Autostraddle*, 18 Jan. 2019, www.autostraddle.com/toys-are-for-us-how-to-start-using-sex-toys-with-your-partner-444845/.

Caputo, Bex. "The Super Powered Yes/No/Maybe List." *Bex Talks Sex*, Bex Talks Sex, 7 Apr. 2018, www.bextalkssex.com/yes-no-maybe/.

Corinna, Heather, and CJ Turett. "Yes, No, Maybe So: A Sexual Inventory Stocklist." *Scarleteen*, Scarleteen, 10 July 2019, www.scarleteen.com/article/advice/yes_no_maybe_so_a_sexual_inventory_stocklist.

Corinna, Heather. "How You Guys -- That's Right, You GUYS -- Can Prevent Rape." *Scarleteen*, Scarleteen, 9 Apr. 2018, www.scarleteen.com/article/abuse_assault/how_you_guys_thats_right_you_guys_can_prevent_rape.

Corinna, Heather. *S.E.X.: the All-You-Need-to-Know Progressive Sexuality Guide to Get You through High School and College.* DeCapo Press, 2007.

Dockterman, Eliana. "Sex Offender Therapy: Inside Treatment With Convicted Men." *Time*, Time, 14 May 2018, time.com/5272337/sex-offenders-therapy-treatment/.

Friedman, Jaclyn, and Jessica Valenti. *Yes Means Yes!: Visions of Female Sexual Power & a World without Rape.* Seal Press, 2008.

Friedman, Jaclyn. "Sex & Consent: It's Time To Go Beyond The Rules." *Refinery29*, 6 Sept. 2018, www.refinery29.com/en-us/sex-consent-laws-yes-means-yes-jaclyn-friedman.

Friedman, Jaclyn. *Unscrewed Women, Sex, Power, and How to Stop Letting the System Screw Us All.* Seal Press, 2017.

Maree Brown, Adrienne. "From #MeToo to #WeConsented: Reclaiming the Pleasure of Consent." *Bitch Media*, 25 Oct. 2017, www.bitchmedia.org/article/the-pleasure-dome/me-too-reclaiming-consent.

Murphy, Heather. "What Experts Know About Men Who Rape." *The New York Times*, The New York Times, 30 Oct. 2017, www.nytimes.com/2017/10/30/health/men-rape-sexual-assault.html.

BIBLIOGRAPHY (Continued)

Nagoski, Emily. "Page 9." *Not on My Watch: a Bystanders' Handbook for the Prevention of Sexual Violence*, by Isabella Rotman, 2nd ed., Isabella Rotman, 2016, pp. 9-9.

Oriowo, Donna. "When We Talk About Consent, Who Are We Really Talking About? - Blavity." *Blavity News & Politics*, 6 Feb. 2018, blavity.com/when-we-talk-about-consent-who-are-we-really-talking-about?category1=community-submitted.

Osworth, A.E. "You Need Help: Here Is A Worksheet To Help You Talk To Partners About Sex." *Autostraddle*, 22 July 2019, www.autostraddle.com/you-need-help-here-is-a-worksheet-to-help-you-talk-to-partners-about-sex-237385/.

"Sexual Assault Prevention and Awareness Center." *Understanding the Perpetrator | Sexual Assault Prevention and Awareness Center*, sapac.umich.edu/article/196.

Silverberg, Cory, and Fiona Smyth. *Sex Is a Funny Word: a Book About Bodies, Feelings, and YOU.* CNIB, 2015.

Washburn, Al, and Archie Bongiovanni. *F*CK ME: A Guide to Getting Off and Getting It On With _______________*. Edited by Heather Corinna, Scarleteen, 2020.

RESOURCES

Sex & Relationship Education

For Teens and Young Adults:

- Scarleteen.com
- *S.E.X. The All You Need To Know Sexuality Guide to Get You Through Your Teens and Twenties* by Heather Corinna

For Middle Readers:

- *Wait, What?: A Comic Book Guide to Relationships, Bodies, and Growing Up* by Heather Corinna and Isabella Rotman

For Young Readers:

- *Sex is a Funny Word* by Cory Silverberg and Fiona Smyth
- Amaze.org

Hotlines

Love Is Respect Abuse Crisis Line:
1-866-331-9474
Or text LOVEIS to 22522*
Chat available at loveisrespect.org

National Domestic Violence Hotline:
1-800-799-7233
Chat available at thehotline.org

National Suicide Prevention Hotline:
1-800-273-TALK(8255)
Chat available at:
suicidepreventionlifeline.org

RAINN National Sexual Assault Hotline:
1-800-656-HOPE(4673)
Chat available at rainn.org

Trevor Project LGBTQ Depression and Suicide Hotline:
1-866-488-7386
Chat available at thetrevorproject.org

Checklists

- A very thorough checklist from Scarleteen: "Yes, No, Maybe So: A Sexual Inventory Stocklist" on Scarleteen.com

- A queer-focused list with great graphic design from Autostraddle: "You Need Help: Here Is A Worksheet To Help You Talk To Partners About Sex" on Autostraddle.com

- A sex toy specific list from Autostraddle: "Toys Are for Us: How to Start Using Sex Toys with a Partner" on Autostraddle.com

- "F*CK ME: A Guide to Getting Off and Getting It On With_____________." A free, printable zine available on Scarleteen.com to fill out and identify the basics of what you really want – if and when you want to enjoy sex with a partner.

- A list with many activities (including kink activities) and response options from Bex Talks Sex: www.bextalkssex.com/yes-no-maybe

Isabella Rotman (writer, artist) is a cartoonist and illustrator from Maine, living and drawing in Chicago. Her art is usually about the ocean, mermaids, crushing loneliness, people in the woods, or sex. Isabella is the author of *You're So Sexy When You Aren't Transmitting STIs* and *Not On My Watch: The Bystanders' Handbook for the Prevention of Sexual Violence*. Isabella is the co-author and illustrator of *Wait, What?: A Comic Book Guide to Relationships, Bodies, and Growing Up*. Isabella has been Artist in Residence at Scarleteen since 2013.

Luke Howard (colorist) is an illustrator, cartoonist and printmaker living in beautiful, sleepy, swampy New Orleans, Louisiana. When he's not coloring graphic novels, he makes sci-fi comics about feelings, and an autobiographical zine called *Abandon Ship*. He's been screenprinting artwork for over 10 years, and spends way too much time fussing with ornery Risograph copiers and greasy offset presses. He loves self-publishing, and has helped organize the New Orleans Comics & Zine Fest (NOCAZ) since 2016. If he's not working, tinkering or organizing, he's probably playing D&D with his friends.

Great Thanks To...

Ari Yarwood, Luke Howard, Amanda Meadows, Heather Corinna, Alfredo Luna, Sage Coffey, Tim Rotman, Lauren Gillette, Laura Fulljames, Andrew Misisco, Ramona Riecke, Jessica Easter, Shawn Morgenlander, Archie Bongiovanni, Kayla Ginsburg, Be Steadwell, Chicago Cartoonist Crit Club, and all the podcasts that got me through this.

THANK YOU EVERYONE!